Stop
the
Yawns

Stop
the
Yawns

A Member's Guide
to Great Talks and Lessons

by

Marcus Sheridan

BONNEVILLE BOOKS™

Springville, Utah

ISBN: 1-55517-654-2
v.1

Published by Bonneville Books
Imprint of Cedar Fort Inc.
www.cedarfort.com

Distributed by:

Typeset by Kristin Nelson
Cover design by Adam Ford
Cover design © 2002 by Lyle Mortimer

Printed in the United States of America
10 9 8 7 6 5 4 3 2 1
Printed on acid-free paper

Library of Congress Cataloging-in-Publication Data

Sheridan, Marcus.
  Stop the yawns : how to become a more effective speaker / by Marcus Sheridan.
    p. cm.
  ISBN 1-55517-654-2 (pbk. : alk. paper)
  1. Public speaking--Religious aspects--Church of Jesus Christ of Latter-day Saints. 2. Preaching. I. Title.
  BX8638 .S43 2002
  251'.03--dc21
                              2002006746

To Mom and Dad

Words give no justice to the positive influence you two have had on my life.

Thank you.

Acknowledgments

I would like to thank my good friends Ryan Aspy, Jon Smith, Talmadge Newsome, Jim Spiess, Jason Hughes, and Thomas Lyon for their help and influence in the production of this book.

I must also thank my best friend and wife, Nikki, for her constant companionship and advice.

Table of Contents

Introduction

A person's ability to grow and succeed is largely related to their ability to suffer embarrassment. —Author unknown

I had my first public speaking experience as a tenth-grader in high school. I can remember the event like it was yesterday. My best friend was running for student body president and he had asked me to read a speech for him in front of all of our fellow class members. Initially, upon his request, I thought little of the matter. Reading a speech that I didn't even have to write in front of a couple hundred people didn't seem too challenging. But when the moment arrived in front of all of my peers, I learned first hand what stage fright can do to someone.

As I stood in front of the audience, my hands shook, my knees wobbled, and the words just didn't seem to want to leave my mouth. In fact, I could barely even breathe, or maybe better stated, my body seemed to forget *how* to breathe. The eyes of the whole student body seemed to be on me. Luckily though, I was finally able to complete the one-page speech. Wiping the beads of sweat off of my forehead, I let out a huge sigh of relief when the speech was finished, and made myself a promise to never get in front of an audience again and relive such an embarrassing moment. I have eaten those words many times since I made that promise.

I was not a member of the Church of Jesus Christ of Latter-day Saints until my senior year in high school. Upon my conversion, I was able to re-confront my great fear of public speaking. This would occur the first time I bore my testimony in a sacrament meeting. Although I only had an audience of about forty on this occasion, I had no script to read. It was just me standing at the podium. The only information I could depend on was the thoughts in my head and the feelings in my heart. My nervousness was still there, but the Holy Ghost helped me just enough to get through the moment. As I sat down after having shared my thoughts, a strange realization came over me: I was invigorated by what had just happened! It had actually felt pretty good.

From that day on, my life has changed in many ways. Eventually I would serve a mission in Chile and become very well-known throughout the mission for my enthusiasm and dynamic talks. I was determined to grow in knowledge and skill with each opportunity to speak. At the end of two years, I knew that I wanted to continue to do as much public speaking as is possible within the Church. Therefore, for the next couple of years while at college, I continued to travel on Sundays as a member of the stake mission presidency and give motivational talks to various units throughout the stake. During this time period, I was also blessed to have my first book published: *Heavenly Father's Angels: The Ultimate Missionary Guide.* Now, at the ripe old age of twenty-four, I am excited to publish a book that has such a demand among the members of our church. To put it in simple terms, I love life! Public speaking and teaching are my passion. And more than anything else, I give all credit to the Gospel of Jesus Christ, which has made me the person I am today. I would never have become a public speaker, nor developed my talents, had it not been for the Lord's church.

Being a Latter-day Saint is much more than sitting down at church on Sundays and listening to a speaker. The Lord has designed His church to help us all spiritually grow together. We accomplish this by speaking to and teaching each others. This is why it is important that every Latter-day Saint become an effective speaker and teacher. If I can do it, anyone can do it. It just takes practice and knowledge. This book is meant to provide you with such knowledge, which will, in turn, enable you to maximize your talents. Whether you are a novice or an experienced speaker, this book can help you. Even though I am the author of this book, I often review its information to remind myself of things I can do better. You will find that as you read it, apply its principles to your talks and lessons, and continue to practice, you will improve greatly. If you already don't have a love for public speaking and teaching, you will find that the application of the principles within these pages will lead you to the utter enjoyment of sharing your thoughts with an audience. Public speaking is one of the most exhilarating as well as spiritually stimulating activities that we can do. It is also a wonderful way in which we can help to build the kingdom of God here on earth. My desire is that you will open your mind to the teachings that are found in this book. I know they work. They are tried and tested. You now have them in your hands.

Chapter One

The Amazing Power of Enthusiasm

Nothing great was ever achieved without enthusiasm.
—Ralph Waldo Emerson

The first few chapters of this book discuss the basic fundamentals that all great LDS speakers have:

1. The ability to show passion and enthusiasm at all times.
2. The effective use of story-telling in sharing personal experiences.
3. Implementation of powerful quotes and scriptures.
4. The ability to speak and act with the guidance of the Holy Spirit.

We are only going to cover the first three fundamentals because there are hundreds of other books available at this time that teach us how to have the influence of the Spirit in our lives. With this being said, I strongly feel that a speaker's ability to speak and act with the spirit of the Lord is much more essential than any technique or skill mentioned in this book.

The majority of the very well-known speakers in our church today share these aforementioned characteristics,

1

including President Gordon B. Hinckley, President Thomas S. Monson, John Bytheway, and Steven Covey. All of these men speak with passion and enthusiasm. They have a clear understanding the effect their enthusiasm will have on listeners. By the time you finish reading this book, I hope that you will share this quality and many others.

The first chapter of my last book is about enthusiasm and how the best missionaries are the ones that are the most enthusiastic. Is this a coincidence? Of course not! The more passionate and enthusiastic you are about the gospel, the more others will see your fire and desire to experience the same feelings in their lives. Enthusiasm has always been contagious and always will be.

Whenever I am asked to give a talk in church, I always choose a topic that I am most passionate about and can relate to. For example, it would be hard for me to give a talk about the impact that Primary has had on my life because I was baptized when I was seventeen and never went through Primary. On the other hand, I enjoy giving talks about missionary work. This is because I was taught by missionaries, I've been a missionary, and I love spreading the gospel news. The next time you are given the opportunity to choose a topic for your next talk in Sacrament Meeting, choose something that gets you excited. If you will do this, you will find the process of preparation and delivery a much more enjoyable experience.

Another benefit of enthusiasm is that it is your best tool to ensure that your audience will not drift off and fall asleep on you. Sometimes I sit in Sacrament Meeting and observe how the actions of the audience directly correlate with the actions of the speaker. Usually, when the speaker is not passionate or enthusiastic, there are yawns, bobbing heads, and blank faces. Conversely, if a speaker is dynamic, uplifting, and confident, I see smiles, attentive faces, and people on the edges of their seats, focusing directly on the speaker. Your goal as a speaker and teacher is to ensure that your audience is in some way positively affected by the things that you do and say. If this wasn't your goal, you would not be reading this book. Here is your first key: Get happy and excited about the subjects you speak about and you will see great results.

What do you think General Conference would be like if President Hinckley stood up in front of the world and did not smile, showed no twinkle in his eye, and acted as if he didn't care about the messages that were about to be given? What kind of tone would that set for Conference? President Hinckley has been embraced by members and non-members around the world because he is a passionate man. He believes in what he says. Even after ninety-plus years of life, he stands tall and speaks to all who will listen. He is eager to tell his message: the Lord's message. Above all, he is sincere in his words. If you watch him talk, you know he follows any counsel that he has ever given. This is what makes him great.

Throughout my travels as a speaker, I have found that not only are enthusiasm and passion critical during a talk, but also before and after. For example, whenever I am about to give a talk, I try to show energy and enthusiasm as soon as I set foot in a chapel. I smile as much as possible, walk with a bounce in my step, and shake hands with every member I come in contact with. I do this for two main reasons: First, these actions fuel the energy and add to the excitement of a talk's delivery. Second, because enthusiasm has a contagious effect among others, a speaker's enthusiasm will help members to get into the proper frame of mind and become excited to hear what the speaker has to say. This is important, because as we will talk about later, a speaker can be stimulated by the energy and participation of his or her listeners.

Now, once the actual talk is over, it is not time to stop being enthusiastic. I once heard a great talk in church where the speaker had the Spirit with him, had incredible skills, and was very enthusiastic about his message. The audience was quite intent on what was being said. After the talk was over, I went up to the speaker, introduced myself, and excitedly told him how I had enjoyed his powerful words. Instead of hearing and seeing the same enthusiasm I had witnessed in this speaker's talk just ten minutes prior, he simply gave me a dull look and said something like, "Oh, well, thanks," and then went on his way. Needless to say, I was disappointed in his lack of interest, which is my lasting memory of this individual, rather than his talk. When I say that we, as speakers, must have enthusiasm, I don't just mean it to be a temporary character trait. It really needs to be a part of who we are and our individual makeup. Everyone has the ability to show energy and excitement, whether it be for a gospel principle or for life in general. It may not come as easy for some as it does for others, but it can be developed over time. It just takes effort and practice.

Once you have become a master at constant enthusiasm in your speaking engagements, you will have won most of the battle. Everything else will fall into place once you have attained this characteristic. Let this be the number one goal you set for yourself while reading this book. Be enthusiastic. Be a motivator. Let your light shine forth. If you do this, you will be a great speaker. It's that simple.

Chapter Two

The Power of Personal Experience

Condense some daily experience into a glowing symbol, and an audience is electrified. —R.W. Emerson

In preparation for this book, I surveyed many church members and asked them who their favorite speaker was. More than half told me they most enjoyed listening to President Thomas S. Monson. I next asked these members what it is they find so appealing about President Monson. The answer to this question has usually been the same—members just love listening to President Monson's stories. I must concur. President Monson is the greatest storyteller I have ever listened to. It seems he has a story for just about every gospel topic. I would say that more than ninety percent of his talks consist of some type of personal experience from his own life. President Monson has mastered the technique of storytelling and he uses this skill to maximize the effectiveness of his talks, thereby making a lasting impression on the audience. When it comes down to it, though, President Monson is just telling us what life has taught him. This is why we are so eager to listen to his words.

This chapter is meant to answer two important questions:

1. Why are personal experiences and stories such a powerful tool for speakers? 2. What skills go into telling a great story?

First, let's answer question number one. In order for your message to hold any weight with your listeners, you must get their attention (via enthusiasm) and then say something that impacts them (a powerful story). Also, your message should have a lasting affect on your audience and not be something that leaves their minds as soon as you have left the pulpit.

For example, let's say you give a talk in Sacrament Meeting, someone comes up to you afterward and says, "I really liked your talk today." Your response is: "Well, thank you for your kind words, Sister Smith. Please tell me what it was about the talk that you found most interesting." At this point you will be able to really tell if Sister Smith was truly impacted by your talk. If she says, "Well, I just thought it was all good," then it is likely that she was just being nice. But if Sister Smith says something like, "Well, that story you told about going to the temple—I could really relate to that," then you'd know that what you have said really did have an impact on Sister Smith. Such should be your goal with any talk.

It always amazes me when a person speaks to an audience for twenty minutes and doesn't share a personal experience. I would compare this to doing the backstroke with your hands tied behind your back. If you have a great tool such as that of personal experience, you must then use it in order to be effective. To understand this better, pay attention to the speakers and the congregation at your next Sacrament Meeting. Observe the difference that occurs with the congregation's focus when a speaker is telling a personal experience, compared to when he or she is giving information. You will notice that whenever a personal experience is told, a dramatic change will often occur within the audience. Heads will pop right up and those few who may have been daydreaming begin to pay attention to what is being said. I have witnessed this hundreds of times. It is truly amazing what a difference a good personal experience or story can make.

Whenever I have counseled members before on this matter, I have often heard the response: "I just don't have any good stories to tell, and besides, no one is interested in my life." People love to hear about the lives of others. Think of all the books, T.V shows, and magazines whose sole purpose is to tell us about the lives of other people. This desire to know about others is also the root of all gossip in our society. If you have had an experience in your life that has stuck with you throughout the years, it is very likely that it will be of interest to others.

In response to the line, "I just don't have any good personal stories to tell," I must again say that we have all had interesting events occur in our lives, it just sometimes takes creativity and energy on the speaker's part to make the story an interesting one. For example, I often use this simple story when speaking to my audiences about becoming spiritually lazy: (Please note that writing this story rather than speaking and acting it out is much less effective, but it should still suffice.)

"One day, not long after I had gotten home from my mission, I was cutting grass with a self-propelled mower at my old house. After having cut most of the yard, I was left with a section of grass that was about twenty feet-by-twenty feet. The grass in this small area had grown very thick and therefore I had to push the handles of the lawnmower in a downward direction so that the front of the mower would come off the ground a few inches. This would cause the blade to be raised up as well, allowing me to go over the thick grass without having the lawnmower cut out on me. As soon a I began to cut the thick section of grass, I noticed that I had gone over a baby turtle. Luckily, though, the turtle had not been touched by the lawnmower's blade because it had been raised up. I was relieved that I had not hurt the beautiful little animal, and placed the turtle in the woods so it would remain unharmed. At this point, I realized that because the grass was so thick in the area I was cutting, I would need to be careful and watch out for any other turtles.

I then proceeded to cut the grass, raising its blade the whole time so that no accidents would occur. After a few minutes, all that remained for me to cut was just one small strip of thick grass. It was only a few feet long and about four inches wide. Because it was so small, I decided to let the front end of the mower down as it would not have any risk of cutting out or running over anything with such a small area to cover.

As I made my final shove, I heard a loud snap come from under the mower. My heart started to beat faster as I cut the mower off and pushed it forward to see what I had hit. My jaw dropped as I saw another baby turtle. This time, though, it had not been so lucky. Its body was torn to shreds. Sorrow filled my heart. Because I had dropped my guard for only a few seconds, I had caused much pain for myself as well as the animal that was left lifeless. As I looked at the baby turtle and pondered what I had done, I promised myself to never drop my guard again. Brothers and sisters, this is how Satan works. He waits until we are in a comfort zone and feel that we do not have to beware of his temptations any longer. No matter how far we have come or what we have done, Satan will always be waiting for us to drop our guard. This is my challenge for you young men and women today: *Keep your guard up and your reward will be well worth the effort spent.*

As you can see, this is a very simple story but the message is extremely strong. I once related this story in a Sacrament Meeting. A member came up to me afterward and said, "Marc, I don't know where you get these crazy stories from, but you sure had me going!" The truth is, most people just forget about incidents that occur in their lives because they feel that they are of no importance. I see it this way: *If any experience that I have had has taught me a lesson in some way, then it will likely teach others as well.*

Now that we have established the general need to use personal experiences or stories in our talks, I have listed eleven important keys for effective storytelling.

The Eleven Keys of Effective Storytelling

1. Use hand gestures and actions. A major key to the effectiveness of any story is the speaker's ability to use hand gestures and actions in such a way that it is easier for the audience to relive the experience with the speaker. I don't care how interesting or exciting a story may be, if the speaker doesn't bother to move an inch and looks as if his arms are tied to the podium, there will be less of a response from the audience. For example, I often tell a story of an experience I had one day when I looked out my apartment and saw two elders in the freezing cold and snow laughing and smiling while they slid down a parking lot. When describing this experience to an audience, I always demonstrate the way the elders laughed at each other and what they looked liked as they slid in the snow. This bit of theatrics has always proven effective for me because I know that when I do this, even the youngest children in the congregation stop their playing and coloring and take a peek to see what I am doing. I am not advocating that one should be doing jumping jacks while giving a talk, however. Everything must be done in moderation and in accordance with what the Spirit indicates.

2. Use names of characters. This is an important aspect of storytelling that many speakers often overlook. Using actual names helps listeners to follow the speaker as well add feeling to what is being said. Take note the next time President Monson gives a talk. When he tells his stories, he *always* says the names of the characters.

3. Don't let your stories carry too long. I have made this mistake many times, as have most speakers. No matter how good you think your story may be, it needs to be kept brief. This way, you will not lose your audience and they will be tuned in to most of what you are saying. I recommend that you keep any story under five minutes.

4. Tell stories that your audience will relate to. This is a very critical aspect of any talk. You must talk at the level of your audience and relate to them in any stories that you may tell. For example, I gave a youth fireside talk shortly after I had returned home from my mission to about seventy-five twelve to seventeen-year-olds. I prepared well for the talk and thought that it would do very well, but I made the mistake of mostly telling missionary experiences that I had had. The talk turned out to be pretty much a dud. I could tell from the audience's reaction while I spoke that they weren't greatly interested in what I was saying. Who can blame them? They were listening to stories that they could not yet relate to. I learned a lot from this experience and haven't made the same mistake since. We will talk more in chapter four about how to relate to an audience.

5. Avoid reading stories from a book. I have seen many speakers in Sacrament Meeting read a story from the Ensign or some other church book. Although these stories are often good, it is better that the speaker read over and become very familiar with the story beforehand. By doing this, the speaker can then give his or her own account of the story, thus making more eye contact with the audience and showing more emotion and enthusiasm at the same time. These actions will help the audience remain alert and interested in what is being said.

6. At the end of each story, make your point. Just as I did in the turtle experience, it is a must that each story is followed by an expressed purpose. This is because most stories resolve at the end, which therefore draws the interest levels of the audience to a peak. A speaker must take advantage of these moments and say something that the audience will internalize. This is also a good time to challenge the audience and admonish them to follow a certain gospel principle.

7. Do not share past transgressions. The Spirit is a very sensitive thing. It comes and goes easily. One way in which it can leave quickly is by relating past transgressions. They are usually an unnecessary element of any talk. Admitting that you are imperfect is fine, but keep the details to a minimum.

8. Fluctuate your tone. This one goes along with making hand gestures. All of the best orators that I have ever listened to are masters at varying their voices in order to make the maximum impact possible on their audience. John Bytheway is very skilled at this. Listening to Bytheway is like riding on a spiritual and emotional roller coaster. This quality helps make him the most sought-after youth speaker in our church today.

9. Be descriptive. Details are very important when telling a story because they spark the imagination of your listeners. Whenever you tell a story, the idea is that everyone in the audience is picturing what you are saying in their head. Details make this picture much clearer.

10. Get excited! We have already talked a lot about enthusiasm, but we must again take note of its importance. Before starting on an experience or story when giving a talk, let your audience know that you are excited share with them the message you have prepared. Also, it is very effective to let them know that what you are about to say is very interesting and they will be affected in some way. For example:

"Brothers and sisters, I am excited to share with you a personal experience that has changed my life. I think you'll find it to be very interesting. . ."

As you can see, it only takes a few sentences to make this important point. Giving an introduction of this manner will draw the attention of the audience and act as a means of building up to the climax and message of the story.

11. Practice telling your stories beforehand. If you practice telling your stories before you actually give a talk, you will be able to work out the "kinks" as well as work on the previous ten keys that we have talked about. You can do this by telling your story to friends, a spouse, or even the mirror. I have often told my wife stories before telling them in a talk or conference. On numerous occasions she has helped me correct simple mistakes that would have been detrimental to the messages of the stories.

If you follow the instructions of this chapter, you will add life and interest to your talks and many positive results will follow.

Chapter Three

Using Scriptures and Quotes Effectively

And the Book of Mormon and the holy scriptures are given of me for your instruction; and the power of my Spirit quickened all things. —Doctrine and Covenants 33:16

Next to being witty yourself, the best thing is being able to quote another's wit. —Christian Nevell Bovee

How would you feel if you were given the opportunity to have the Savior himself participate in your next talk or lesson? What would you say if Alma offered to be a guest speaker for your youth group in a fireside about missionary work? Better yet, what would be your feelings upon knowing that Joseph Smith was willing to share a few words at your next Gospel Doctrine class? Once you have contemplated these questions and gotten excited about their possibilities, I would like you to understand that all of these scenarios are still possible in our church today. We have the means of using these wonderful servants of the Lord whenever needed. They are always within an arm's reach. How is this possible? Through the scriptures, of course!

What a wonderful tool the scriptures are. Although the

use of scriptures and quotes usually takes up very little of the actual time we spend in front of an audience, they can have a monumental impact on the direction as well as the overall effectiveness of a talk. We'll discuss why we use quotes and scriptures in this chapter and also the ways in which we can use them more effectively.

As members of the church, the words of the Lord and His servants are very important to us. They lead and guide us and affect each and every one of us in different ways. They teach, inspire, guide, and motivate. Their beauty and influence are endless. With such power, it is a must that we take advantage of them. After all, scripture is the Lord's word. He is the best teacher of all. If you, as a speaker, can bring the scriptures to life for your audiences, then you have impacted them in a very positive and profound way. This can be difficult to achieve, but with the help of the powers of enthusiasm and the Holy Ghost, it can happen. I have listed five keys to effective use of scriptures and quotes in talks:

The Five Keys to Properly Using Scriptures and Quotes

1. Share scripture background. I have heard countless speakers share scriptures without telling their audiences anything about the history or background of the text. This can be damaging to the impact of what the scripture is saying. For example, let's say you are teaching a group of new members a lesson on obedience. You would like to use 1 Nephi 3:7 to make your point, and therefore you decide to:

A. Have a class member read the scripture and then have the class comment on it, or. . .

B. Tell a brief background history on where 1 Nephi 3:7 was derived from. Include the fact that when this statement was made by Nephi, he had already left Jerusalem, walked hundreds of miles, listened to the murmurings of his brothers, and faced many more sufferings in order to the flee into the wilderness with his father, just to be told to return to Jerusalem in order to obtain the plates of brass. After explaining to your class the scripture's background, you then tell them to contemplate how the verse is applicable to us in these times. Finally, with everything prepared properly, you have a class member read 1 Nephi 3:7 and then ask the class members how they feel the verse relates to their lives.

Can you see the difference in the two scenarios? In the first one, no preparation is done in order to help the class understand what is happening. With this method, there is very little thought provocation, which leads to uninterested listeners and a lack of learning.

In the second scenario, Nephi's background is well-described, and class members can therefore imagine what it would have been like to be Nephi, hear his father's desires, and then follow his command. With such knowledge, 1 Nephi 3:7 will undoubtedly have more of an impact on the class.

The idea of explaining the background of a scripture is nothing new, but it is often overlooked by most members, including myself. This practice can be used very effectively in both lessons and talks.

2. Keep your focus on only a few scriptures.
The next time you are listening to General Conference, count how many different scriptures the speakers use in their talks. If you do this, you will find that most speakers use two to three scriptures per talk. This is because the more you read scriptures during a talk, the more likely your audience will tend to drift off and lose interest in what you are saying. If you focus on just a few scriptures, you will be able to spend more time conversing with your audience, which is really what they want. We should not use scriptures as time-fillers. They should only be used to give a talk direction and balance. A speaker's personal experiences, stories, and thoughts are what should make up the majority of a talk. It is often effective and necessary to use more scriptures when teaching lessons, however, depending on the allotted time of the lesson and the subject that is being taught.

3. Add emotion. Can you imagine Nephi, who was "large in stature," saying in a sheepish voice, "I will go and do the things which the Lord hath commanded. . ."? Of course not! The reading of scriptures often requires a little bit of theatrics and imagination.

For example, if you were to read 1 Nephi 3:7 in a talk, you would want to use a strong voice as well as your hands and arms to show emotion, trying to act as Nephi would have acted in that moment. By doing this, the scripture will have more impact on the audience. Also, their ability to imagine what Nephi was doing and saying will be greatly enhanced. The scriptures were not meant to be read in a sheepish or monotone voice. They were meant to be spoken with power and authority.

4. Take your time and use pauses when necessary. The next time you read a scripture or quote in a talk or lesson, read the words slowly. This will give your listeners time to digest what you are saying. The same idea applies at the end of the scripture. After reading the passage, pause a few seconds and you will notice that many members of your audience will have a look of thoughtfulness on their faces. This is exactly what you want. Also, if you feel it is necessary to stress a scripture or quote to your listeners, repeat the passage. Doing this will give your audience more of a chance to contemplate the message you are trying to get across.

5. Do not overload a talk with quotes. I really enjoy a great quote. A quote is a tool we have as speakers and teachers to arouse the interest of our listeners, and can be very effective, humorous, and thought-provoking. In fact, there have been various C.S. Lewis quotes used in talks by church leaders. Despite the potential effectiveness of quotes, they should not be used too often.

I once gave a talk that consisted of seven of my favorite quotes. I was excited to read and expound them with my audience but by the time I shared three of the quotes, my audience began to lose interest. By the seventh quote, I noticed many wandering eyes and blank faces. This incident taught me a great lesson. The old anecdote, "Too much of anything can be harmful" comes to mind when I think back to this experience.

Although there is much more to be said about the use of

scriptures and quotes as a speaker, this chapter should give you a solid base. By combining the use of the Holy Ghost, enthusiasm, story-telling, scriptures and quotes in your talks and lessons, you will be using the greatest tools that we have been given to uplift and inspire our fellow men.

Chapter Four

The Audience/Speaker Relationship

You may use different sorts of sentences and illustrations before different sorts of audiences, but you don't—if you are wise—talk down to any audience. —Norman Thomas

In the previous chapters, we have talked about the characteristics of great speakers: enthusiasm, powerful storytelling, and the effective use of scriptures and quotes. Before we move on and analyze talk preparation and delivery, we must focus on one other major aspect of any talk or lesson: the relationship that you have with your audience. What importance the audience holds for a speaker! No talk is a good talk without the help of a lively and participating audience. *What is a lively and participating audience,* you may ask. It is one that is focused on the speaker—alert, and excited to know what will be said next. A participating audience is one that is more worried about hearing the message of the speaker than they are about looking at the long hand on the clock. Many speakers often forget the fact that audience participation is crucial, and end up falling short in their efforts to impact their listeners. This chapter consists of keys that will help you to better understand as well as maximize the audience/speaker relationships that you will have in the future.

As we have already established, you are reading this book to be the best speaker you can be. With such a desire, you will want to do everything possible to positively impact your audience. In order to accomplish this, you will have to use many techniques that will enhance the relationship that you have with them during a talk. As I have studied audiences and speakers throughout my speaking and teaching experiences, I have found that there are basically two types of audience-speaker relationships. I have dubbed them the "Happily Married" and the "Not-so-Happily Married" relationships. Whenever you give a talk to an audience, it is similar to marriage because you are going to be with each other for an allotted time whether you both like it or not. This can be a happy time, or a difficult time, depending on what you both do. You, though, will set the course and tone of this relationship. It will be your job to keep the other entity happy, excited, and interested in what you have to say. The best speakers and teachers will always find ways to light a fire in their audiences. The great thing about this "marriage" relationship is the fact that as a speaker, you can feed off the energy of your audience. Their actions and responses to your words can quicken your thoughts and enhance your abilities. At the same time, your actions as a speaker will basically determine the interest level and over all awareness of your audience. Simply put, when you are together, you are better. So let's talk about this marriage and all that we can do as speakers to ensure that it is a healthy and prosperous relationship.

Ten Keys to a Healthy Speaker/Audience Relationship

1. Speak at the level of your audience. There are few things worse than listening to a speaker who uses words and phrases that are beyond the level of his or her listeners. This happens often, mainly because speakers sometimes feel that more extensive phraseology invites more interest from the audience. They also feel that this makes them look impressive. This is a myth. A great way to lose the interest of your audience is to use words and phrases that are beyond their comprehension. As speakers, a goal should never be to impress others with our abilities.

2. Select topics your audience can relate to. Can you imagine giving a talk to a youth group about the importance of starting a 401k plan? Such a talk would be almost impossible. As a speaker, you must talk about subjects that your audiences can relate to. If you do not, your "marriage" will quickly be on the rocks. This is why you must do your best to address their interests and concerns, and not just yours.

3. Learn to drop names. It is an excellent idea to utilize the names of your listeners in your talk. When an audience knows that one or more of them is actually involved in "the act," they perk right up and wait to see what else the speaker will mention about them. People just love to hear positive things about themselves. This is a sure fire way to connect with your audience.

4. Learn about your audience. As with dropping names, this works great in cases where you have been asked to speak at a ward or branch to which you don't belong and know few, if any, of the members. If you want to get the interest of your audience, say something about them that they had no idea you knew. This will be sure to fascinate them and increase their willingness to listen intently to your message.

5. Show your appreciation. The act of appreciation goes a long way in life, especially in a speaker/audience relationship. Show appreciation for their kind acts, and they will be more inclined to take your words to heart. Openly criticize them, and you might as well take a seat.

6. Identify with your audience. If you would like to quickly gain the support of your audience, tell them of something that you both have in common. This simple act will arouse their interest and lead to better audience participation.

7. Make your audience a partner in your talk. This technique is most commonly used in teaching lessons, although it can be used in talks as well. Asking questions, taking polls, having listeners stand up, and asking a member of the audience to come forward to participate in a demonstration, are just a few ways that you can form a partnership with your audience.

8. Show a sense of humor. One of the few universal expressions that all people show is the smile. There is nothing compared to the knowledge that something you have said has made another person smile, laugh, or feel good inside. A great way to accomplish this is to show a sense of humor. Don't be afraid to make others laugh. Also, do not be afraid to laugh when you are speaking. This simple act will show others that you are a fun person to be around. It is also important to note, though, that not all talks and lessons are meant to be funny. Depending on the subject matter and what the Spirit indicates, one must distinguish between times of laughter and times of seriousness.

9. Play yourself down. A great way to lose your audience is to act as if you are better then them in some way. For example, let's say you are going to give a talk on tithing. It is not a very good idea to start your talk by saying, "I have chosen to talk to you all about tithing today because I have paid my tithing in exactness every month of my life and there is no excuse why you all cannot do the same thing."

Such a statement indicates that the speaker in one way or another feels that he is more righteous than his audience. A great example that we can find in the scriptures of "playing yourself down," as well as many of the other audience keys that we have talked about, is that of King Benjamin. In his final major discourse given to the people of Zarahemla, he states, *"I have not commanded you to come up hither that ye should fear me, or that ye should think that I of myself am more than a mortal man. But I am like as yourselves. . ."* (Mosiah 2:10-11). We can see here that King Benjamin had a clear understanding of how to relate to his audience and play himself down. Let us all follow his example.

10. Love your audience. To put it in simple terms, love is a great motivator. This is why we can feel the love our prophets have for us whenever we read or listen to their counsel. If you sincerely love your audience, your message will be more powerful and the hearts of you listeners will open more easily.

These keys are very important. Apply them to your talks and lessons to the best of your abilities and you will see incredible results with your audiences each and every time you are blessed enough to be asked to expound on the Gospel of Jesus Christ.

Chapter Five

Talk Preparation

Spectacular achievement is always preceded by spectacular preparation. —Robert Schuller

Okay, you have been asked to give a talk. Great! This will be a wonderful opportunity for you to learn, grow, and progress spiritually. Also, it should be a fun and enjoyable experience. Remember that when you are preparing your message. This chapter focuses on how to prepare for a talk, the steps that are involved, and ideas that will make the process a more pleasurable and easy experience.

In our church, there are basically two types of talks. I have dubbed them the "assigned" talk and the "just speak on whatever you would like" talk. If you ever have the option to choose your topic instead of having someone else decide it for you, be sure that you do so. This will enable you to speak on a subject that you are most passionate about. It also gives you the opportunity to speak on a subject in which you hold some type of expertise. If you do have the option to speak on a subject of your choice, I suggest that you not only ask yourself what you would most like to talk about, but also to pray and ask the Lord what He feels His sheep need to be taught. If you have already decided on a topic, you can even confer with Him on the subject that you have chosen to speak. Doing this will give you even more confidence and enlightenment on the subject matter of the talk. Once you have chosen or been given a topic to speak on, whether it be tithing, charity, prayer, fasting, or any other, your next step is to form a basic outline for the talk. This outline will be used as a guide and map as you share your message. For many people, the process of forming a talk outline is a very difficult one, but it does not need to be this way. The following six steps that I have listed are meant to be easy, efficient, and practical for any speaker:

Six Steps to Forming a Talk Outline

1. **After receiving the topic of your talk, think of as many experiences that you and others have had with this topic.** These experiences are very important and will make up the body of your talk, so reflect on your life as well as the lives of others. If no experiences come to mind, it is very helpful to research the church magazines, especially the Ensign. If you have the Internet, it is a great idea to take advantage of the Gospel Library on **www.lds.org**, the church's website. This site is full of helpful information on just about any gospel topic imaginable. As you think back to the experiences that you have had and research the words of others, write down any information that you feel could be pertinent to your talk.

2. **Select two to four of these experiences or stories that could have the most impact on your audience.** If you are not sure which stories to choose

from, just choose your favorites. Which experiences have impacted you the most? If the stories are interesting and pertinent to you, then they should have that same effect on others.

3. Uncover the lessons behind the stories. Once you have selected the experiences or stories that you would like to share, discover the lessons you learned from these events. Again, record your general thoughts on paper.

4. Focus on the talk's objective. Now that you have thought of the lessons learned from these experiences, understand that these lessons form to make the goal, or objective, of your talk. For example, if you learned from certain experiences that it is always a good idea to listen to the promptings of the Spirit, the objective of your talk could be to help others to listen to and obey the promptings of the Holy Spirit. Of course, with each story that you have chosen, there can be a variety of lessons learned. Just remember, every story and every scripture read should support the overall objective of the talk.

5. Find the right scriptures and quotes. Now that you have established a basic body and goal of your talk, research scriptures and quotes that will support and add meaning to your admonishments. A good idea is to use one scripture or quote with every story. This way, the audience will hear evidence from three different sources— the story, the scripture or quote, and the speaker. This proves to be very effective.

6. Write the outline. Now that you have the basics (stories and scriptures), all you need to do is put these ideas down on paper by writing out a talk outline. I have listed one of my talk outlines to give you an idea of what these six preparation steps should look like.

Sample Talk Outline

Subject: Missionary Work

Overall Talk Objective: Help members get excited about missionary work and desire to apply the principles taught in their own lives.

Introduction: My love for missionary work, my conversion story.

Lesson #1: Attitude and enthusiasm are very important.

Scripture #1: D&C 123:17 (as said by Prophet Joseph Smith while he was in Liberty Jail) "Therefore, dearly beloved brethren, let us cheerfully do all things that lie in our power. . ."

Story #1: How my attitude affected the success I had as a missionary.

Lesson #2: The Lord will help us in times of need when we attempt to share the gospel.

Scripture #2: D&C 33:8 "Open your mouths and they shall be filled, and you shall become even as Nephi of old. . ."

Story #2: How my companion and I overcame the problem of an empty baptismal font to have a spiritual baptismal service.

Lesson #3: There are chosen and prepared people in any area. There is no such thing as a "dead" area.

Story #3: The success my companion and I had in an area that was supposedly "tracked out" and lacking of potential converts.

Quote: "There is no such thing as good or bad, but thinking makes it so." —Shakespeare

Closing and Testimony

What I have listed is basically the same amount of information that I bring up to the podium whenever I give a talk. I do not write much down on paper because all that I need is an outline that will keep me on the right track. Too many papers and books can cause clutter and confusion. This is also why I write out the scriptures or quotes that I am going read. Using this method will cause the majority of the talk to be a conversation between myself and the audience, hence the word "talk." This method is also very relaxing for a speaker. With its flexibility, one can use creativity as well as any promptings of the Spirit that he or she may feel during the course of the message.

Once you have come up with an outline, practice telling your stories. Whether it be a story from your own life or a story that you have picked from an Ensign, you need to become very familiar with saying the story out loud. This is best done by practicing with a friend or relative or by simply talking to the mirror. When you practice telling your stories, be sure to use details and gestures as we talked about earlier. Always ask your listeners for feedback and look for ways of making your stories more clear, concise, and powerful. By doing this, you will feel more confident and comfortable when the actual talk arrives.

Practicing your stories will also give you a good idea of the length of your talk. If you notice that your stories and thoughts carry on too long, this is your opportunity to make adjustments. Stay within the allotted time that you have been asked to speak. It is inconsiderate to take the time of another speaker.

The principle of practice and repetition also applies to any scriptures or quotes that you have selected to use. Read over these words of counsel many times. Ponder and pray about what they are saying and you will likely receive additional inspiration as to what to say in your talk.

One last word of advice. **Do not memorize a script.** This is not done very often, but for some reason, it is still an occurrence.

What is wrong with memorizing a talk? First of all, it is an extremely difficult and time-consuming task. Second, most people end up having to read from their scripts because they get flustered in front of an audience and lose their place. Third, memorized talks are usually mechanical, lacking in emotion and enthusiasm. And finally, people want to hear words that come from your heart, not from the storage banks of your brain. This is also why it is usually less effective to write your entire talk out on paper. By doing this, you greatly lessen your ability to speak from the heart, follow any promptings of the Spirit that you may feel during the talk, or grab the attention of your audience.

I have kept this chapter short for one main reason: As I said earlier, the preparation that a speaker puts into any talk should be an enjoyable and uplifting experience, not a grueling and mind-boggling journey. If you will stick to the admonishments of this chapter, you will find that the six steps mentioned here work. I have used them many, many times and am sure of their results. By following these steps and writing out an outline, you will have all that you need for a very successful talk.

You may have noticed that I have not discussed actual preparation time for a talk. This is because there isn't a set time for quality talk preparation. Some of my best talks have been prepared in twenty minutes. I have also had experiences where I have prepared days for a talk, only to fall on my face. My point is that as long as the talk outline is well done and has been diligently practiced, the message will most likely be very effective, no matter how long or short the preparation time is.

Chapter Six

The Talk

The way to develop self-confidence is to do the thing you fear and get a record of successful experiences behind you. Destiny is not a matter of chance, it is a matter of choice; it is not a thing to be waited for, it is a thing to be achieved.
—William Jennings Bryant

After you have done all that you need to do to prepare your talk, the day arrives when you must present your thoughts to an audience. This can be a great experience or very forgettable experience. Everyone has good and bad talks. There are many factors that decide the over all effectiveness of any talk and this chapter is meant to help you understand more in depth the factors that will make your talks consistently great.

How to Control Your Fears and Nervousness

I cannot remember the last time I gave a talk and was not nervous. Nervousness is a fact of life for any speaker. All the way from President Hinckley down to Joe Primary, members experience some type of nervousness when they have to give a talk. In fact, public speaking has always been listed as one of society's greatest fears. However, people who overcome this fear greatly improve their self-confidence and sense of well-being. In life, each time we learn to conquer our fears, we are actually conquering many more battles down the road with which we have yet to be confronted. This is one of the greatest aspects of the Lord's church. He wants us to develop and improve on our talents. Giving talks in Sacrament Meeting or teaching a lesson does exactly this. As I mentioned in the introduction, I have very strong testimony of the fact that we can develop our talents as we actively participate in the Gospel of Jesus Christ. What a blessing this is!

One must also understand that stage fright and nervousness can actually be useful to a speaker. For example, I recently gave a Sacrament Meeting talk and was pretty nervous before sharing my message. My heart was beating fast and I found myself breathing a little harder. Did this bother me? Of course not, mainly because I understand that as a speaker's heart beats faster, they can more easily show enthusiasm as well as be spiritually inspired in the things they say on their feet. Remember this the next time you experience nervousness before you have to give a talk. Use this nervousness to your advantage and you will be surprised at the great results.

When it comes down to it, stage fright is just a natural part of the speaking process. No matter how seasoned a speaker you are, nervousness is going to be present. If you are a novice speaker, take this advice to heart and plow through your fears. Each time you experience success, your enjoyment for speaking will grow. Instead of agony, the thought of sharing your thoughts and experiences becomes a pleasant and pleasurable experience. In fact, the day I stop being nervous is the day I stop speaking, for I know that if I have no sense of anxiety, my talks will be lifeless.

Give Yourself A Pep Talk

In the days, hours, or minutes before a speaker gives a talk, it is common to have some type of apprehension. "Am I prepared enough to share this message?" "Is this the right topic for my audience?" "What if my thoughts become jumbled up and I sound silly?" "How can I get up in front of all these people?" These are just a few of the possible questions that can run through a speaker's mind. In such times, a speaker must combat these thoughts with a good pep talk. In clear and concise terms, tell yourself that the talk you are going to give will be great because it is derived from your own thoughts and experiences. No one else could share these experiences like you could, and you may take comfort in knowing that you have chosen the perfect talk for you. This is what matters most. It is a proven fact that the power of autosuggestion is one of man's greatest tools to combat fear and reach new heights of greatness.

Take A Deep Breath

A classic result of nervousness is distorted breathing patterns. Take it from me when I tell you that trying to give a speech without breathing is a difficult task to complete. To understand what I am saying, the next time you read your scriptures see if you can make it through one entire page on just one breath. This is why it is important to breathe deeply before giving a talk as well as during the talk. In fact, take about a minute just before you give your next talk and focus on taking long, deep breaths. This has been proven to relax the body, stimulate blood flow, and reduce nervousness.

The Introduction

Finally we get to address the actual talk, starting with the introduction. Although the introduction does not take up the majority of a talk, its influence is monumental. This is because it sets the tone of the entire message and affects the mood of the members of the audience as well as the speaker. I have listed seven tips to an effective introduction:

1. Once you are standing, look at your audience and pause. When used at the right time, silence can be a powerful tool for speakers. This is why it is a great idea to start off your talk by standing at the podium and looking out at your audience without saying anything. Make eye contact. Look over the whole congregation. This should only be done for about two or three seconds, but you will find that it is an excellent attention grabber.

2. Never start with an apology or negativity. I am sure that you have heard a speaker start off his talk with a statement like, "I have been so busy that I have not been able to prepare this talk as much as I would like."

Or "Well, the bishopric asked me to speak and despite the fact that I don't like giving talks, I said that I would speak today." As a listener, do you feel such statements enhance the effectiveness of a talk? The answer, of course, is "no."

Despite this fact, so many talks are started off with some type of excuse or negative comment. Such statements have no place in any type of talk or lesson. They do nothing to enhance the speaker's goal or invite the Spirit. All that they do is discredit the speaker and lessen the effectiveness of the message being shared. Also, if you are nervous, there is no need to mention it to everyone. This will only make the problem worse because it draws attention to any nervous behavior you may be exhibiting.

3. Be enthusiastic. Are you noticing that enthusiasm keeps coming up throughout the course of this book? I cannot stress its importance enough. You don't have to start off your talks jumping up and down, yelling and screaming, but you do need to show that you are genuinely excited to have the opportunity to share your thoughts to a wonderful group of people.

Express your anxiousness to share the message you have prepared. Tell the audience that you appreciate the opportunity that they have given you to speak to them. Statements like these will establish an upbeat mood and initiate a sense of excitement among your listeners. These statements will also help to invite the influence of the Holy Ghost. Notice this technique the next time you listen to General Conference. Every speaker initiates his talk with some type of enthusiasm and appreciation.

4. Give your audience a preview of what they are going to hear. Just like any good movie or television show, it is a good idea to give your audience a preview of what you are going to talk about. This can be done in just a few lines. Here's an example:

"I am very excited to have this opportunity to speak to you on this wonderful day. I'm also thrilled to share with you a few experiences that I've had that have changed my life."

As you can see, this preview is very basic and simple, but it gives the audience something to look forward to.

5. Share a little about yourself. This is especially a good idea when you are speaking to an audience who does not know a whole lot about you. By sharing with your listeners a few facts about yourself, you are able to build a relationship of trust with your audience and therefore have the chance to impact them even more with the message you have prepared.

6. Bear your testimony. Sharing your testimony in the introduction of a talk can be very effective in bringing the Spirit to your words. Saying a sentence as simple as, "I testify in the name of Jesus Christ that the things I am going to speak about today are true" is very, very powerful and will grab your audience's attention.

7. Sharing jokes at the beginning of a talk is not required. Although I do not oppose telling a joke at the beginning of a talk, I want to note that there are many other ways for a speaker to "break the ice" with his or her audience. I usually prefer to share a funny or interesting story about myself. I have found this is more effective than a joke because it is an icebreaker, attention-grabber, trust-builder, and tone-setter, all in one.

The Body

In the previous chapter, we covered most aspects of what the body of an effective talk needs. As long as you use personal experiences or stories, show enthusiasm, and utilize scriptures and quotes, you should be very effective. Remember to bear your testimony often, especially at the end of each story and be sure to speak at the level of your listeners.

This also applies to the stories that you share. Tell them in such a way that they can be beneficial to all listeners. Also, focus on the members of the audience that seem most tuned in and interested in what you are saying. This will increase your confidence, concentration, and ability to speak effectively.

The Conclusion

Just as the introduction is short yet important, the same applies to the conclusion of a talk. The conclusion is important because it is your last chance to make a great impact on your audience. I have listed four keys to an effective conclusion:

1. Always bear your testimony. Whether you have shared your testimony twenty times or not at all during the talk, always bear a strong testimony at the end. Say it with force and with power. Draw upon all of your faculties to express the feelings you have about the topic you have expounded on as well as your testimony of the Savior and His church.

43

2. Do not shuffle papers. I see this all the time with speakers and I am sure that you have seen it many times yourself. At the end of their talks, just when they are sharing their final testimonies, they begin to straighten up papers, close their scriptures, and stack everything up in a pile. This is detrimental because it is not only distracting, but it also causes the speaker to look down at the podium instead of looking at the audience. The next time you give a talk, wait until "amen" and then begin to put everything away.

3. Don't hesitate to share a final story, quote or scripture. This is a good way to finish with a bang and leave your audience with something to remember. Accompany it with testimony and you will have capped off an excellent talk with a powerful ending.

4. Leave your audience with a challenge. Throughout the talk, you have focused on having your audience understand a gospel principle more clearly through the words that you have spoken and the spirit they have felt. All of this has led to the point when you leave the audience with some type of challenge that relates to the overall objective of your talk. As human beings, we love challenges. We thrive on them. Without them, we fall short of our potentials. This is why every talk should consist of some type of challenge from the speaker to his or her audience.

You now have all of the information you need to produce a great talk. Apply what you have learned so far and I promise that you will reap the benefits.

Chapter Seven

A Closer Look at President Monson's Speaking Methods

Now that we have covered what the characteristics of a great talk are, we are going to see these characteristics be put to use by one of the most powerful and moving speakers in our church today, President Thomas S. Monson. As I mentioned in Chapter One, in order to prepare for this book, I surveyed many members and asked them who it was that they most enjoyed listening to. More than half of these members said they most enjoyed listening to President Monson. Therefore, after hearing so many comments from others about President Monson, I decided to take a closer look at his style and the characteristics of his talks. The results I discovered were profound, and run parallel with everything that we have talked about in this book.

To understand President Monson's style better, we are going to analyze a talk that he gave in the October 2000 General Conference. This address, entitled "The Call To Serve" can be found in the November 2000 issue of the Ensign, starting on page 47. If you have access to this Ensign, I recommend opening up to this talk so you can have an even clearer understanding of President Monson's speaking characteristics.

45

To start off the address, President Monson states, "What a privilege is mine to stand before you tonight in this magnificent Conference Center and in assemblies throughout the world. What a mighty body of priesthood!"

You may have already noticed a few attributes of this introduction that coincide with the counsel given in this book. First, President Monson stresses that it is his "privilege" to speak to such an audience. Immediately, he is putting himself on the same plane as his listeners as well as expressing sincere gratitude for the opportunity that it is for him to speak to this group of people. President Monson also demonstrates his enthusiasm and passion in this introduction as he says "What a mighty body of priesthood!" It is obvious that he is excited about the topic for which he has prepared.

After his initial statements, President Monson reads a scripture to give his talk direction and thereby informs his listeners that he will be speaking on the subject: The priesthood. Following this scripture, President Monson then reads a quote by President Wilford Woodruff which discusses the power of the priesthood.

Before we continue analyzing this talk, let's review all that President Monson has done in just the first three segments: He has expressed equality and appreciation to his audience, enthusiasm for the topic, read a scripture to give the talk direction, and a related quote to add further light on the topic of priesthood.

Following the introduction, President Monson shares a personal experience from his childhood of when he was ordained a deacon. This short story is well-expressed and uses powerful details to enhance the imagination of the listeners. Immediately after sharing this experience, he bears his testimony to the young men in the audience and also shares a quote from the Stanford University Memorial Church (notice how President Monson even gives the names of *places*, and not just people). A few paragraphs later, he shares another story about a young man he knew as a bishop, whose name was Robert. The story involves Robert's triumph over his stuttering in order to perform the baptism of Nancy Ann McArthur (Notice how President Monson always uses the names of the characters in his stories). Immediately following this story about Robert, President Monson again bears his testimony as to the importance of providing our youth with faith-promoting experiences. Throughout the remainder of the talk's body, President Monson shares two more personal experiences, one involving his first talk in church and the other dealing with an experience he had while in the navy, each story terminating with his personal testimony.

What have we learned up to this point? First of all, we can clearly see that President Monson has a great understanding of the power of personal experience. He knows that his audience will take interest in and relate to the stories he tells. He also understands that the best way to teach is by sharing with us what the world has taught him. He comprehends the importance of bearing his testimony at the right time, and this is why he exhorts and bears his testimony after each story told.

To close his talk, President Monson shares a letter that he received from a farmer regarding President Hinckley. Before reading the letter, though, he gives his audience a preview of what they are about to listen to. He says, "I close by reading a simple yet profound letter that reflects our love for our prophet and his leadership." President Monson then shares the short, powerful letter and even mentions the name of the individual who wrote it. This leads him to his final statement, one of love and admiration, as he says, "President Hinckley, we the priesthood brethren of the Church do love and sustain you. I so testify, in the name of Jesus Christ, amen." What a beautiful conclusion to an incredible talk!

Truthfully, if someone wants to be a great speaker and teacher, all he needs to do is follow the example that President Monson has given in this talk. Throughout this book, I have reiterated that the characteristics of a great speaker are the ability to show enthusiasm, share personal experiences and stories, utilize scriptures and quotes, and form strong relationships with an audience. President Monson demonstrates all of these skills throughout the talk's entirety. In fact, as far as talk content is concerned, Monson relates to us a total of five personal experiences, reads three scriptures, and utilizes four quotes.

In Chapter Two there is a list of eleven keys to storytelling. In this particular talk, President Monson used ten of the keys mentioned in this chapter. The only one he did not use was that of putting action in stories, which is pretty difficult to do when speaking at General Conference. Chapter Three tells us of five keys to sharing quotes and scriptures. I count the use of four of these keys in President Monson's talk.

Concerning the ten keys to a healthy speaker/audience relationship found in Chapter Four, one can find that President Monson has used all ten of these keys! Now can you see what makes him such a great speaker? This does not even include the fact that he is a spiritual giant, which, as we have already established, is the most important characteristic that a speaker can have.

The majority of President Monson's talks are just like the one we have analyzed in this chapter. He always demonstrates enthusiasm, tells powerful stories, utilizes scriptures and quotes, and forms a strong audience/speaker relationship. These qualities help make him one of the greatest speakers of this dispensation.

Chapter Eight

Effective Gospel Teaching

Now, at a time when our prophet is calling for more faith through hearing the word of God, we must revitalize and re-enthrone superior teaching in the Church.

—Jeffrey R. Holland

We have a challenge. Our challenge, at least from what Jeffrey R. Holland has told us, is to be superior teachers of the Gospel of Jesus Christ. How can we do this? And what exactly is *effective gospel teaching?* For starters, the church tells us that the role of a gospel teacher is, "to help individuals take responsibility for learning the gospel—to awaken in them the desire to study, understand, and live the gospel and to show them how to do so. . . The learning has to be done by the pupil. Therefore it is the pupil who has to be put into action" (Teaching, No Greater Call [1999], 61). Can we meet this challenge? Of course we can! And we will. This chapter is meant to help you to be the best teacher you can be. It consists of fifteen do's and five don'ts that are meant to guide you whenever you are blessed with the opportunity to teach a lesson in church. Although we could probably write a whole book on the do's and don'ts of teaching, I want to stick with some of the basic keys that will lead to success. It is also very important to note that everything that we have talked about in this book up to this point can be applied to lesson-teaching. The only major difference between a talk and a lesson is the fact that in a lesson, the audience participates (hopefully) much more and the teacher speaks much less. It is that simple. Also, remember that the key to any great lesson is the influence of the Holy Spirit on the teacher and the class members. Again, this should always be your number one goal.

The Fifteen Do's of Teaching an Effective Gospel Lesson

1. Show enthusiasm. Here we go again with that "E" word. But seriously, we could never talk enough about the importance of enthusiasm. A teacher must be enthusiastic and passionate about his or her topic. This is what keeps students awake, on the edge of their seats, and excited to come to class.

2. Talk less. I have seen many great speakers give ineffective lessons. Why? Because teachers often forget that class members are there to participate, not just to listen. In order for everyone in a class to be edified, all must participate in some way. This cannot occur if the teacher is speaking the whole time.

3. Always have a clear idea of the lesson's objective and stick to it (unless the Spirit otherwise indicates). Everything that is done or said in your lesson should in some way deal with your lesson objective. If someone, including the teacher, gets off track, the lesson will lose focus and therefore will not be as effective. This often happens when a class member digresses. Although this cannot always be prevented, it is your duty as the teacher to get everyone back on track.

4. Prepare diligently and prayerfully. If you are not prepared, your class members will recognize this immediately and therefore lose interest in the lesson. You want to give them the impression that you have worked hard in preparation for the message that you are about to share. This impression leads to respect and more effort from the class.

Also, take advantage of the power of prayer on behalf of the teacher. By doing this, the Lord will enlighten you as to what you need to do and say to help the members of your class.

5. Ask thought-provoking questions that invite discussion. The greatest teachers are the ones that let the class members teach themselves. This is accomplished when thought-provoking questions are asked (stay away from "yes" and "no" questions). Also, when you ask questions, sometimes it is a good idea to ask for a specific class member to respond. Although you don't want to embarrass anyone, some students need a little motivation to participate.

6. Show love and appreciation. Love will always be a great motivator and teacher.

7. Use stories and examples. Just as we have already talked about, if you have learned something from an experience, your class members will likely learn from this experience as well.

8. Use pictures and objects. It is a proven fact that the human mind remembers pictures and objects much better than it does words.

9. Use activities. Activities are great because they stimulate learning by providing a change of pace for the class members.

10. Bear your testimony often. Not only is it important to bear testimony at the end of a lesson, but also throughout the lesson. A teacher can also ask class members to bear their testimonies on a certain topic. This is a great way of inviting the influence of the Holy Ghost.

11. Always provide students with positive feedback. A good way to make your class members feel embarrassed is to not say anything positive when they have brought up a point. No matter what their point is, it is you job to respond in some type of positive manner. This will also increase class participation. Some examples of possible responses to a class member's comments are:

Thanks for the comment.
I like how you put that.
That sounds very interesting.
You bring up an important point.
Thanks for your input. Let's see what the scriptures tell us about this matter.
That sounds interesting. Could you explain further?
I think I'll write that one down!
What a great idea!
Now we're thinking!

12. Know your class members. As a teacher, you should do your best to know the names of your class members and any other pertinent information about them that will help you to motivate them to learn and apply what they learn. Also, the more interest you show in your class members, the more interest they will have in the things you teach.

13. Teach at the level of your audience. We talked all about this in Chapter Four. Great teachers know how to adjust their lessons according to the levels of their class members.

14. Always review with class members what they have learned. It is a great idea to do this at the beginning and end of each lesson. At the beginning of your lessons, ask class members what they learned about in the previous lesson. Also, inquire if they have applied anything they learned in their lives. At the end of each lesson you teach, ask class members what it is they have learned and what they will be taking with them once the class is over.

15. Ask for feedback from class members. One must have thick skin in order to do this, but with thick skin comes self-improvement. Your class members, especially if they are youth, are usually willing to give you feedback on your teaching skills. Ask them what you do well. Find out what you could improve on. It is just a matter of you being able to ask for their thoughts and suggestions.

The Five Don'ts of Effective Lesson Teaching

1. Don't make excuses or apologize. No one has ever been uplifted by hearing a teacher say that he or she had not had enough time during the week to prepare the lesson. Making such a statement is like saying, "I have many priorities and this class is just not one of them." If you have made the mistake of poor preparation, just keep it to yourself.

2. Don't bury your face in a lesson manual. If you are looking for a sure fire way to bore your class members to death, just look down at your teaching manual and read from it the whole lesson. This provides little opportunity for creativity, enthusiasm, and class participation.

3. Don't demean or embarrass your class members. No one wants to be embarrassed. Embarrassment and hurt feelings are what cause members to go inactive. It also causes hard feelings, and when there are hard feelings present, the Spirit is absent.

4. Don't give your own doctrine. As a teacher in the Church, it is not your job to share your opinions on doctrinal matter that has not been disclosed. Stick with the basic facts of the gospel. For example, let's say you are giving a lesson on the Second Coming. There is absolutely no reason to tell your class members when exactly you think the Second Coming is going to happen. To say that the time is near is fine, but to say that it will happen in 2020 will do nothing to enhance the objective of the lesson.

5. Don't get discouraged. Not every lesson that you teach will be perfect. We are all on the same path, striving to do what is right and working toward our own individual perfection. This process will take time, and there will be many bumps and obstacles along the way. All that we can do is learn from our mistakes and plow forward. I have never taught the perfect lesson nor given the perfect talk, and I doubt I ever will, but I know that by applying the information found within these pages, I will speak and teach to the best of my abilities, just as you will too.

About the Author

Marcus Sheridan is quickly becoming a well-known self-help author in the LDS market. He joined the LDS Church at age 17 and is the only current church member in his family.

Marcus served in the Osorno, Chile Mission from 1997-1999. While there he experienced great success in bringing others to the gospel. His methods of missionary success are shared in his first book, Heavenly Father's Angels: The Ultimate Missionary Guide, which he wrote while completing his bachelor's degree at West Virginia University.

Marcus currently lives with his wife and daughter in Virginia, where he serves as a counselor in the Bishopric and teaches the Gospel Doctrine class. He is also a noted speaker at Especially For Youth events.

Marcus enjoys comments from his readers and can be reached at **marcus_sheridan@hotmail.com**